THE ALANICUS

Theodore
Bishop of Alania

Translated by: D.P. Curtin

Copyright @ 2020 Dalcassian Press

All rights reserved. No part of this publication may be reproduced, distributed, or transmitted in any form or by any means, including photocopying, recording, or other electronic or mechanical methods, without the prior written permission of the publisher, except in the case of brief quotations embodied in critical reviews and certain other non-commercial uses permitted by copyright law. For permission request, write to Dalcassian Press at dalcassianpublishing at gmail.com

ISBN: 979-8-3302-6298-4 (Paperback)

Library of Congress Control Number:
Author: Curtin, D.P. (1985-)

Printed by Ingram Content Group, 1 Ingram Blvd, La Vergne, Tennessee

First printing edition 2020.

BISHOP THEODORE OF ALANIA
LETTER TO THE BISHOPS IN CONSTANTINOPLE AND THOSE LIVING THERE,
which, due to the events of the times, are somewhat shortened.

THE ALANICUS

I. What the purpose of our journey has been, I know you have long desired to understand, both before and now, most especially, great shepherd, and after the first time recently, as well as you, fellow shepherds; what indeed has been the outcome of our long pilgrimage, what has been done in it, but especially how the Spirit has led us; by whom, although not always stirred. We have been, now certainly after he has bestowed the anointing upon us. Therefore, have we found a more fortunate journey, and have we come straight to our flock? Or, having fallen into the hands of robbers, should we flee for the sake of preserving our lives? What is the state of affairs, and has it turned out well enough for us? Has the onslaught of fortune finally ceased, or are we still in the midst of it? And which of these two should we hold on to? Have we completely missed the mark so far? It is your task to consider these things and discuss them among yourselves. I certainly think it is a serious matter, worthy of no small concern, if anyone wishes to examine our affairs more closely. However, as is often the case with such matters, any other interpretation, and nothing that has been sufficiently proven publicly, is spread by popular rumor. If indeed I had so much leisure and convenience, I would say and write everything, even though I would take particular care to tell a better story for the sake of mutual comfort and the affection of my listeners. But now I cannot do that, because it would require a long discourse from me. And to expend effort in writing would be as if one were to elegantly adorn himself with weapons for a night battle and thus proceed. But I could not do that at all, my mind still wandering while I begin to learn barbaric things. Even though these things would not force me into silence, the narrative would create an intolerable dizziness, just as a man from the Mediterranean Sea experiences nausea at sea, and as delicate and soft drugs have an effect.

II. Moreover, desiring you, o father and assembly of brothers, whom the Holy Spirit gathers together even though distant, I do not know how to conceal a matter among our well-known ones. And is this perhaps Joseph here? For it is clear that the patriarch Jacob mourns the last of his sons, who is still an infant in spirit; and therefore we are loved. So the elder brothers cultivated the harvest of life, and I myself was dedicated to the ministry, ready to devote myself as the father had commanded. However, they sold me, moved by some twisted instinct of the mind: but certainly, this was a tragedy, unlike the old one. Yet I know myself, although in shadow and not without a veil. For I pass over many things. Nor do I command the Egyptians through Pharaoh anymore, who, although he refuses to yield to any power, is still persuaded by the one who sends visions and dreams by the spirit. Indeed, the sense yields to the intellect, instructed by him to understand whatever it receives through symbols. For the night of the world does not comprehend the truth. But let us do these things that are sent.

III. Therefore, to describe the entire journey from the beginning is beyond the scope of this time and the duty of speech; and how much the third sun has seen us endure. Indeed, we have briefly mentioned some of these to those who ask, narrating them in passing, unless these perhaps have escaped your curiosity. The first guardian of the roads troubled me, pursued and captured me, and divided the spoils, although he did not satisfy his own greed. The second devastator, even more maliciously abundant, but nevertheless did not prevail. For God once again performed those famous miracles: He divided the sea, led defenseless men, not so much pursued by the enemies as already being caught by them, which is of greater value. He struck the second in rank with a blow: for even among us was the most confident Paul, the apostle of the Gentiles, who considered all things as worthless compared to the Gospel, burning with zeal, knowledgeable in the mysteries of the Spirit, my shepherd, indeed more of a spiritual father than a physical one. Snatched away from chains just like Peter, we passed through the first and second guard. But as is the custom of divine dispensation, He temporarily relented so that greater miracles would soon be performed. We have briefly explained these things; and we believe that no one will be found who, if they inquire, will not see them as clearly evident.

IV. Furthermore, Cherson and the Scythian region know the events that took place here, which kindly treated us as travelers, upon hearing about our misfortunes. For after he who had rendered the malice of the wicked ineffective persuaded our tyrant to act against his own will, he expelled us exiles and the city allowed us to be free.

However, this did not please him, and he sent wicked messengers to the authorities, and added harsh words. And indeed, without any prohibition, they allowed the citizens to use us as they pleased. But God was present, restraining, and He moved one of the nobles of Cherson, a man entirely equal to the famous John: who, however, did not grant the freedom to flee from danger, because he feared the attack of the people, lest he be killed by that bloodthirsty man, and that the people who were being driven by external forces from all sides would turn against him. Thus, he kept me in between freedom and chains. And what about the one who accomplishes everything by his own will alone? For he was also a fiery furnace, a new Egypt, and Israel held captive by a free man, and Moses, the knower of the mysteries of the ancestors. For he too was sent to free me from the clay and brickwork, even though Pharaoh ruled harshly against it, and in the presence of
By divine prodigies, the exterminator was near; and the city bewailed its own misfortunes: for outside, the swords of the foreigners were restoring it to its desolate state, while inside a civil war was erupting. However, we did not immediately take flight.

5. Nor indeed did that lost man stop here, truly worthy of the left side. But since we were exiles not far from Chersonesus in the Alanic region (for the Alanic people are quite scattered, extending from the Caucasus mountains to the Iberians, which was their ancient homeland boundary; they also tend to send out some colonies, so that they have filled up almost all of Scythia and Sarmatia); there he also pursued us with his cunning and schemes, even attempting to bring about our death: for there was nothing else left. So he rushed here. The hated Deo threatened war against Chersonesus and the Pasillians Alans, unless they surrendered to us. This Tzamanes was so shamelessly ridiculous by nature and unworthy of anything, except insofar as he was full of malice and a servant of the Devil. Furthermore, he was ignorant, wise only in wickedness, and not worth a straw, not realizing that we were apostles of God, for I boldly say that God works miracles for us. For he who divided and gathered the Erythrean Sea, saved the fugitive people, and at the same time drowned the persecutor in the waters, he divided this city into parts, inciting war both civil and foreign; and this division gave us an opportunity to escape. But God brought the city back to concord, so that the one who sought tyranny was almost lost, had he not sought his safety in flight. So much for that.

VI. But the evils inflicted upon us even in sacred war must also be recounted, as they exercised tyrannical force against us; a matter that can be called nothing other than a wicked conspiracy: indeed, a tower of blasphemy was raised high under the guise of dignity. And indeed, it was almost on the brink of a confusion of languages; or there was an attack of ignominy by some priests against Elijah. For there was a zealot among us, although the spirit also killed him with a sword. Or against Jerusalem, the Assyrian army dangerously attacked itself, not returning safely. The situation was such that we briefly narrate the calamity. The Alans also live near Chersonesus, no less sought after than willing, to be around that city as a kind of wall and guard. I saw them, very cheerful, running to their native shepherd and surrounding him, wanting us to stay with them, not omitting any kind of duty. And we, in turn, used words of exhortation for them to live worthy of the calling of Christ. They were (I am not ashamed to say, nor will I refrain from some offense) a wandering flock in the mountains and desert places and pits, having neither a sheepfold nor a pen, so exposed to the devouring of wild beasts; for there was no one to provide pastoral care for him, even though many desired it. Moreover, it would not have been allowed even for those who wanted to; because he was not yet in a suitable condition. They had recognized that he was a bishop; although Paul, the great trumpet, the teacher of the nations, and therefore ours. But they think that the bishopric is something delightful, and devoted to worldly cares.

VII. Do you know the bishop of Cherson? Why then should I speak many words to those who are already aware? This old and aged bishop seemed to be dying to himself, because the Alans were among us, or rather because we were dwelling in Cherson. Immediately the conversation turned to the boundaries of jurisdiction, and that the bishopric of the place was his own, while my office was temporary and foreign. These are the known pretenses of today's bishops; namely, the foreigner who held his own country; the guilty, the one who was the judge, omitting the rest, as is fitting.

IX. But truly, after we had obtained some part of our freedom, we thought about the way, according to the goal each one had for his journey, and we headed towards the Bosphorus. Indeed, there was fear of the harsh winter weather, and the presence of the Scythians around the Bosphorus was an obstacle: nevertheless, we set out on our journey, even though we might lack success. Who can tell of Scythian troubles? Who can mourn enough for what we have seen or suffered? But indeed, neither did the helmsman cease to steer the ship, nor did he stop navigating, despite the winds opposing us, until he had brought the ship into port. The same was our goal; therefore, once again the care and preparation for the journey: and again the former hardships as companions. And with us indeed traveled sickness, and poverty that usually accompanies it, and deviation from the intended goal. Furthermore, I endured things as they presented themselves; but I compelled my father to return home again. And what then? The old bishop alone, when finally he came to the Bosphorus with his sons.

X. And behold, another calamity and affliction: for he was not received by the prince. You all know that ancient evil, the old and first enmity; and what is more serious, and expresses tears from the heart, the shepherd and the flock were nearby, to the extent that they saw each other: and indeed he made a lamentable sound with the flute to invite them; and the flock indeed wanted to run to the shepherd and surround him; for they heard and recognized his voice; and yet they could not. They say that the whole city came together to the powerful man, saying that they wanted to either die or receive their bishop: however, because he was swayed by him, whether the old man was crying, or the strong man, or the wailing boy, or the lamenting woman, or the entire city was distressed and mournful. Why, I ask? Because envy consumed the man, and because he was harsh and obstinate, not obeying the princes according to custom. And if he acted untimely and absurdly, it is a serious matter and not in accordance with the usual practice to be praised by us. But rather bravely and strenuously, as we have heard of the deeds of ancient men, let us be with them whatever the circumstances may be.

XI. After we were indeed prohibited from approaching there, to another much larger and rougher place, whatever we might suffer, we turned towards the region. And indeed our father remained there in the meantime among a small number of Alans, bearing all kinds of hardships, poverty, insults, and abuse. For not everyone is capable of understanding their speech; and they become judges of those who are mainly in charge of judging; and what is worse, they condemn them. But we, having advanced into the middle of Scythia, traveled a total of sixty days, poor men, and deprived of all necessary things. However, this was tolerable, because not far from the first apostolic journey we departed; and by the grace of your God. With the approval of food, O father and brothers, the desired companionship and name are seen by me, we see the flock, a matter most dear and esteemed above all to me. Why not? Since this inheritance is from God to me, and indeed the best.

XII. So far, my speech has flowed easily, and has proceeded in almost its own order. But what remains, I would prefer to leave for another day, and keep silent myself; for neither does my tongue allow me to speak, nor does my hand provide easy work for writing. Alas for me, because my sojourn has been prolonged, so that we may have already perhaps entered into accursed days, in which even the Antichrist himself may emerge. For now his smoke has touched us with its biting moisture. Hence I have begun to weep, and I do not cease from weeping, and I dare to say that I will not stop! Alas, now our evils have begun, and perhaps for the first time the furnace of ultimate calamity will be ignited for us, kindled by tiny sparks! Will it not immediately seize the trees, since Satan has also subverted the faith of the sincere? Alas for me, because we have become as if in the beginning, when you did not rule over us, says the Scripture! Alas for me, because on the foundation of the apostles, straw and reeds were built, and they were immediately consumed by fire! Oh, who here, lamenting, will weep for us like the prophet of old wept for Jerusalem! Surely neither I, nor you who are present, nor my speech is false; no, I say; through this furnace, I swear by the calamity which I have received in the midst of my soul.

XIII. When I come to this part of the conversation, I am moved only to tears, and I am disturbed by sorrow, without knowing who I am, or what kind of story I will tell: but I feel that I will only narrate the matter abruptly. For I am greatly disturbed, and it is not possible for the mind to control the soul: "The shepherds," says the Scripture, "have destroyed my vineyard... But now false shepherds have disgraced the desirable portion of Christ. And I do not hesitate to affirm that in deserts and in places lacking the living water of doctrine, and where the beautiful feet of the evangelists could not reach, the rose of faith bloomed, barely irrigated by the first moisture of preaching. Hence, perhaps we ascended to the love of Him, to reveal the unknown matter to many, and to explain the controversial cause of this pilgrimage: namely, that we might cultivate a barren field with sweat on our faces, and that we might again be able to build the summit of life, or the ancient condemnation. May God grant it! if we have undertaken the task with a not relaxed mind, kindling the flame of zeal.

XIV. However, time has brought many things that can easily be enumerated by no one. For the vicissitudes of things are always being renewed over time, but it has never presented anything equal to this. From a certain anonymous region and through a harsh winter, a spirit of ignoble unbelief stirred, disturbing the sea of peoples. He ruined the ship of the Church, lacking a captain, now in light hope, endangering in the abyss of despair. Alas! Alas! What a crime! How can I possibly narrate the matter? For I feel it to be truly unbelievable. Indeed, the church of the Alanians was stripped of its head honor, sacred, I say, by that pastor, who least of all lied about the apostle: for there he ended his life, having performed his duty splendidly. There was also a certain wicked protector, shameless, as they say, waging war for her with a bare head. And his arts and devices usually ignite the rage of avarice in some who provide him with their service, especially pretending the simplicity of the people, the difficulty of the times, and that the Alan people were easily deceived.

XV. Indeed, there was a man among them, mentioned above, not obscure in birth, reaching that pastor. He begins a plan worthy of his head, and truly ill-considered. For taking with him, as if with that demon already defeated in the Gospels, seven other demons. surrounding the pastor were wolves, and what is surprising, men unworthy of his conversation, some of whom were fugitives from elsewhere, and had nothing healthy at all; and also a certain man emerging from some corner of the Lazars, seemingly well-dressed, and not having an indecent beard, as they say; this man, I say, finding the Alan church cleaned with brooms, and that man who fills everything with good spirit empty; he enters with free foot, and the last things become worse than the previous ones: for even those were not quite healthy. Therefore, with what words shall I narrate the most wicked man's invasion, and with what footsteps he stood, and what he found not unworthy of the service of more honorable men? Grant me pardon, you who are present, to one having a troubled mind, and guide the prayer in a straight course for the powerless. And indeed, hastily, in this pain of the soul, and due to the uncertain course of various business, I see that I have not yet said anything: for I was forced to keep many things silent; thus it happens that both I and everyone will be involved in perplexity. In the meantime, those excellent ones enter;

and indeed that pestilential Lazas is called a bishop: but these openly and

XVI. Therefore, at the very beginning, like a certain Egyptian plague, it attacks; except that here it was the first, which there was the last and more severe. For the firstborn, which was consecrated to God, this exterminator was going around. And there was no wise Moses present to explain the mystery of his ointments, namely the blood of the Lamb; nor any protection, but complete extermination. For the thief comes to steal, slaughter, and destroy. Woe to the wickedness that I saw, obscured by the neglect of what is right! For if the head of the household had been vigilant, the thief would never have dug into the house. Do you want me to enumerate somewhat the actions of his pastoral life? For what is that of Paul? The precept is that hands are not quickly imposed on anyone. But this man, within a few days, like a priest examining ants, sent out twenty of them, they say, arranged by him as if by a passing horseman, murmuring a few things between their teeth not understood by anyone, and certainly not uttered with their lips. He fed fifty others while he was at the table and held a cup; others while he lay in bed at night. Indeed, there are those who affirm with a dire oath that he did not even rise from the bed. But why should I inquire further? These things are not easy for me to say, but intolerable for you to hear? Finally, after these actions, he fled to Lezica, eager for his axe again. He is not, I think, an unknown man to some merchants who go there. They demand rewards because they did not allow the Alans to be without a shepherd, but with all patience and labor they have rewarded the bride with such a free gift.

XVII. I feel indeed that many questions will be stirred among you who hear this conversation. But some will not allow themselves to be persuaded; which I acknowledge well, as I compare mine with yours. For even I did not immediately believe when I heard; at first, I understood these things leisurely, and then I learned many things by questioning. But it was so easy to deceive the willing; and thus the sheep followed the wolf, as if they had never seen a shepherd, nor heard his voice. But what? Was not this excellent shepherd here for the last two or three days? Did they not know about his disorderly bishopric? Certainly, this fact was not obscure or unclear to many; although not to all, certainly to the priests who received ordination from him. Therefore, it must be one of two things: either they did not know, which is unbelievable because those who could be ignorant were those who experienced it? Or, otherwise, that is, they knew the matter; and why did they neglect such an important matter of anointing and think they were receiving grace from one who had no soundness? Especially since there are some who saw the succession of three bishops, and now I am the fourth; I was explaining the insignia of the high priesthood to them, whether obvious in clothing or in the attire of the altar, which were openly displayed to all so that they could recognize the bishop from there. I was also enumerating the steps by which one is promoted who is a priest. The point is going to be important. These things, I say, and many others like them were persuading me not to believe that I had heard the matter accurately and safely; but I blamed my ignorance and held those telling such things in contempt. But after hearing the words, I recognized that I had not applied faith rashly.

XVIII. Therefore, should I not seem to deprive my speech of confusion, to rightly refine my address to you? However, such a law is not established for those who speak. I would have preferred you to hear these things from someone else rather than from me, and thus to place the speech again in hiding; but I would not dare to publish this matter in writing. Moreover, I have not learned to act as my own accuser; nor do I wish to judge, obeying the admonition of the Gospel; for where speech is swift, there also condemnation takes flight. In the meantime, these things have taken place, and in this manner of kindness our flock has received us. Outwardly threatening, that sword was ready to deprive us of our children on both sides. For the land of the Alans was envying us, and fear was emerging as if from a storehouse. Indeed, I was turned in fear, unable to figure out how to handle these things in my situation.

XIX. What do you think I, a timid priest ignorant of the pastoral art, would have endured in such circumstances? That elder Daniel sits as judge of the elders, condemning the guilty with shameful violence; and she, having suffered violence, avoided condemnation. Where is the spirit of Daniel? And yet our situation was more violent. For our Susanna suffered a greater loss of modesty, partly due to the ignorance of her helper, partly due to his absence. Oh wretched me, a man experiencing a heavy yoke immediately. Or rather, is the yoke indeed sweet and the burden light, and I, in my stubbornness, have resisted it, and therefore have not recognized its lightness? For he who does not bear the cross on his shoulders and is immersed in worldly laziness, how can he bow his neck and commend his spirit to the Father? Since even before a stable foundation in goodness is established, the cup is offered and baptism. The cunning enemy, the ancient adversary, seeks the just man; for he could not tempt him there, but he deems a man who is inherently foolish, even more desirable. But if such an adversary is accustomed to succumb to weaker and lighter struggles against us, how great will be the onslaught against great athletes, truly running in the stadium of the spirit?

XX. As for me, I completely fell into perplexity: for I could not look to just anyone for such a matter; neither was any father present, nor an older brother, proven in doctrine and experience, who could provide counsel. And the matter was clearly beyond my understanding, and truly needing your, O father and brothers, spiritual discretion. Nor did I myself not know, although I had not known that he would undertake any such work. And I diligently delayed, until not without prudent experiment, the support of their common judgment who preside over the Gospel. But the barbaric attack, and the insane force, and the necessity of the matter, and my unfortunate absence from you, as from Abraham's bosom, weighed heavily on my late distress. Indeed, I will tell you the reasons, if you wish to hear: If that ordination which is believed to be in vain, I said, then ordain canonically. But if you refuse to do so, let those who consider themselves ordained in any way fulfill the priesthood. But he will by no means bear this, I said, nor will he allow those who carry it out with a great spirit to fulfill the priesthood. Why then should I hesitate to ordain, and fear that I might seem to ordain again? which the sacred law forbids: For whatever the law says, it says to those who are under the law, and therefore repeated ordination, as long as someone has been ordained canonically before, is not recognized by us. Who would think that ordination is valid if it is not received with grace to be imparted in return?

XXI. And these things happen in passing, as sacred doctrine teaches. But what is even more absurd, it seemed to them to be enough, even though someone might be deceived here. Not because of this, but because they fell into a violation of the law, embracing a profane priesthood: and indeed they whispered things that are of the spirit to the deaf and carnal. However, it was not so much their insane violence that moved me, but the urgent necessity of the matter: "For the harvest is plentiful," says the Gospel, "but the laborers are few"; whoever may say that this harvest is abundant, and whatever oxen the laborers may be. For I have heard that even those patriarchs who had bread for themselves and food for their cattle were once pilgrims. And indeed, that good farmer does not reject us, though we are devoted to the body and the earth; he assigns shepherds to flocks, and fittingly one to the other. For such a harvest, such laborers. Therefore, I was so prepared that I would do nothing without your advice.

XXII. But because there was no intermediary way, and the urgent business was pressing; for a danger was looming over the community of the Church, all being so weak, and with no one suitable for the priestly office now standing (I say this, and you forgive me): not without examination, nor lightly, but finally I laid hands on them, teaching them first to condemn their former opinion, and to placate God with works of mercy to the best of their abilities; and I did not ordain everyone, but only those whose life did not contradict their dignity; finally, what is more important, I indulged their ignorance, making up for whatever was lacking in greater perfection. If these actions were perhaps not done worthily, correct me with your forgiveness; I profess to have striven to be among your disciples. But if I ask late and after the fact, what should I do? when I was burdened by distance, necessity, and perplexity in these matters? However, it is clear that when I ask now, I will not even omit that: nor would I have done anything before asking, if indeed it were unclear. Why wouldn't I ask now after the fact? But whether this matter is not entirely in line with your purpose and spirit, decide for yourselves." And let these things be so.

XXIII. But what evils the people of Alania nourish, who am I that I was compelled to heal them with my preaching? For if I am destined to present the chosen people to the Lord, why do I gather figs from thorns, or grapes from a bramble bush, as Scripture says? Now I understand the gospel parable, when the seed is indeed good, but still impure weeds grow up from it: besides that, laziness intervenes after the sowing for them, but for us it is worse. It happens that in the very act of sowing, a defect arises. Then the other parts of the parable also agree: in the thorns, the sowing takes place, which indeed were once uprooted; but the word of faith is completely choked somewhere: sometimes it even grows with the thorns themselves: likewise, perhaps, by some kind of affection, it becomes thorny itself. Surely it would be better if we were to immediately burn the thorns from the one who comes to send fire into the earth inflamed; if by the help of him who also comes to send a sword into the earth, we were to completely cut these down. And indeed, pure earth, pure seed, vigilant guardians, a golden harvest, a sturdy reaper. However, as things stand now, I do not indeed demand that the powers of virtue be extended to a hundredfold; nor do I wish to be carried to the sixtieth, but I am content if, as far as physical rules allow, the work yields a thirtieth of the fruit. Indeed, I fear that perhaps, while reaping, I may fill my hand, but not the lap in which I gather the sheaves. I am indeed slower than others, although not entirely despairing, an unhappy shepherd not blessed. Indeed, we who sow over the roofs have made little profit, namely by gaining those who have avoided the mother of all evils, and have harvested the word to the best of their abilities; unless perhaps the birds of the air have also laid traps for them. Alas for me, because the field is sprouting thorns and thistles! Indeed, damnation is the result of straying from God, while the wandering flock follows a thorny error; while it commits fornication not only on wood, as it is written, but also on all stones and waters; while they do not worship idols, but certain demons in high places.

XXIV. They are called Alans by the name of Christians. But if there is any part of Jacob somewhere, the enemy has sown weeds. Even in old age, Sara gave birth; but Ishmael persecutes Isaac. And who is Abraham, who will drive away the servant Hagar and the servile shadows of heresy from afar? I also have a small army, which God rescues from the intellectual Pharaoh. With this one as my leader, not indeed as another Moses, but still as a leader. Behold! The Egyptian tribunes pursue, namely the mind eagerly desiring to be beaten, and the foolishness of earthly things; which urge me to defile myself with foreigners; finally, the oblique agility of the mind towards certain absurd opinions, not resisting as is usually the case. And where is the cloudy pillar, which provides separation? Or how did the sea withdraw from the nations? Alas for me, to whom it is entrusted to feed the flocks ascending from the bath of baptism! Rather, death feeds them on unbelief. Indeed, with difficulty I say, they confess with their mouths for salvation; yet they do not believe in their hearts for righteousness beforehand. It is similar to this: The religious one has perished from this land of mine; nor is this a place of rest for me.

XXV. Shall I then rise and go? I fear to part in this evil. For am I not Abdias? Indeed, while he was serving Ahab, he did not bend his knees to Baal. I also fear the fate of the righteous; for the rod of the wicked is stirred up. What shall I do? Where is the whip of Jesus, to cleanse the Father's house? I hate the church of the wicked: but I was cast into it, daring to take on the priesthood recklessly: "Did I not hate those who hate you, O Lord, and waste away upon your enemies?" Why did I boldly expose myself to that curse? I am considered a pillar of salt, my inheritance is a land neither plowed nor sown. Who will give birth to these again, until Christ is formed in them? They are still bastards and not sons, for Satan has bewitched them, lest anyone should believe in the truth, and so they may become sons of unbelief. I fear the wrath, for truly there are vessels of wrath formed for destruction. Alas! I see the teeth of beasts, raging with fury upon the earth! For the emblems of mine are like, chiefly murders and other kinds of deaths. Alas, Dathan and Abiram gape at me: and who is like Aaron, to perform God's miracles? The dignity of the priesthood is trampled, and who is like Samuel, to reckon the injury inflicted as if upon himself? "For they called upon the Lord, and He answered them: He spoke to them in a pillar of cloud." Indeed, I seriously observe the custody of sacred testimonies. Perhaps someone may also mock my baldness, if I should perhaps remove my hat, so that I may perform the sacred duty with unveiled faith. Who will be like Elisha to follow soon after with vengeance for the sin? I will boldly say I am a disciple of Elijah: but I am not therefore Elisha. And indeed, I have received grace, but not therefore am I outside the assault of transient things, nor have I entered into peace beyond all disturbance of the soul. And why wonder, if Moses is again the leader, and yet the limbs of those journeying have fallen in the desert? For many are called, but few are chosen.

XXVI. But how long will I extend my speech in these matters, and not rather reach that goal? Namely, to ask my shepherd, and at the same time beseech my brothers. Surely from the depths of the underworld they will hear my cry. Lift your eyes to God, o father: stretch out holy hands, from which you have asked for the grace of priesthood for me. Now ask that I may complete the course, keep the faith, teach the ways of the Lord to the transgressors, convert the irreligious: if ever the Lord grants us these benefits. Bring help in this to your father, most beloved brothers: commend me to the common and chief shepherd, who I need to be ruled by rather than to rule. Perhaps he who keeps the little ones will remember his wonders: perhaps he will bring to mind his works, who turns dry land into springs of water. For if he dries up the rivers of Ethan, and turns fertile land into salt marshes, he nevertheless gives honey to suck from a rock and from hard stone oil. Who knows, whether from a nettle and useless herb, myrtle and cypress will rise up? Just as he who again joins dry bones, and breathes life, may he also be glorified in us. This is my request to you: so with tears I will not cease to implore. Grant me this grace, agree to this request, vessel of choice, O God, O first among all after the first, O lights of the world offering the word of life.

The Scriptorium Project is the work of a small group of lay people of various apostolic churches who are interested in the preservation, transmission, and translation of the works of the early and medieval church. Our efforts are to make the works of the church fathers accessible to anyone who might have an interest in Christian antiquities and the theological, philosophical, and moral writings that have become the bedrock of Western Civilization.

To-date, our releases have pulled from the Greek, Syriac, Georgian, Latin, Celtic, Ethiopian, and Coptic traditions of Christianity, and have been pulled from sundry local traditions and languages.